HAKEEM OLAJUWON

JANE PRETZER MARSHALL likes reading, good basketball games, watching birds, playing the drums, being a mom, vacations, and her job. She is features editor for the *Houston Chronicle*. She and her family live in Houston, Texas, home of the back-to-back NBA Championship Rockets.

GOING FOR THE GOLD

HAKEEM OLAJUWON

JANE MARSHALL

AN AVON CAMELOT BOOK

GOING FOR THE GOLD: HAKEEM OLAJUWON is an original publication of Avon Books. This work has never before appeared in book form.

AVON BOOKS
A division of
The Hearst Corporation
1350 Avenue of the Americas
New York, New York 10019

Copyright © 1996 by Jane Pretzer Marshall
Published by arrangement with the author
Library of Congress Catalog Card Number: 96-4129
ISBN: 0-380-78677-X
RL: 4.9

Library of Congress Cataloging in Publication Data:
Marshall, Jane, 1945–
  Going for the gold—Hakeem Olajuwon / Jane Marshall.
      p.   cm.
Summary: Describes the career of the Nigerian-born basketball player who brought the Houston Rockets its first NBA title and has now become an American citizen. 1. Olaju-won, Hakeem, 1963–   —Juvenile literature. 2. Basketball players—United States—Biography—Juvenile literature. 3. Houston Rockets (Basketball)—Juvenile literature. [1. Olajuwon, Hakeem, 1963– . 2. Basketball players. 3. Nigerian Americans—Biography.]
I. Title.
GV884.O44M37 1996   96-4129
796.323'092—dc20   CIP
[B]   AC

First Avon Camelot Printing: June 1996

CAMELOT TRADEMARK REG. U.S. PAT. OFF. AND IN OTHER COUNTRIES, MARCA REGISTRADA, HECHO EN U.S.A.

Printed in the U.S.A.

OPM 10 9 8 7 6 5 4 3 2 1

To Clara and Hannah

Contents

Birthday in Nigeria

On the flat grasslands of northern Nigeria, an elephant roars.

In the palm forest near the Niger River, a monkey screeches at its baby.

In the tangled mangrove swamps near the Atlantic Ocean, a tiger-heron fishes for dinner.

In Lagos, the biggest and busiest city in Nigeria, Salam Olajuwon steps out into the morning. Many people on the streets around him wear Western clothes. But Salam is dressed in the traditional loose flowing robe of his ancestors.

A hot dry wind blows from the Sahara Desert on its way to the Gulf of Guinea. It is called *harmattan,* and it stirs clouds of dust around the city. But the dust does not disturb Salam.

Today is a special day. His wife, Abike Olajuwon, gave birth to a son on January 21, 1963. Today the baby is a week old. Today the baby receives his name.

Salam walks back into the room where Abike holds their infant son. Around him the local Islamic teacher, called the *imam,* and friends prepare for the naming ceremony. Abike and Salam have chosen a name. Following Islamic tradition, they have told no one but the *imam.*

To begin the ceremony, the teacher recites the Arabic call to prayer to the baby. Then he reads special verses from the Koran.

He announces the baby's name. This is the first time the name has been said aloud.

After the ceremony, Salam looks down at his child. "Welcome, Abdul Hakeem Ajibola Olajuwon," he says. "Hakeem. The wise man. It is a good name for such a son."

Yemi Kaka and Kudirak creep closer. Kudi is one year old. She is no longer the baby in the family. Shyly Yemi reaches out to touch his baby brother.

"You can play with him when he is a little older," Abike tells her young son, touching his tightly curled dark hair. "Hakeem is a very big baby. And he is as handsome as an emperor, just like you were when you were born."

The proud parents look at their new son. They touch his long-fingered dark hands. These hands will hold greatness. They touch his large sturdy feet. These feet will take him far. As they look into Hakeem's dark eyes, they see something special.

They know he will change many lives. They know he will be honored by many. He will do great things to serve Allah and make them proud. But they do not know he will grow to become a legend known to people all over the world.

Soccer Star

Hakeem sat in the small hot classroom, his legs folded tightly under his desk. He tried to concentrate on his English lessons. He loved learning, almost as much as he loved soccer. He was curious about this strange language with funny sounds and words with many meanings.

Teachers told him that in England and America, people speak only English. They do not speak Arabic at prayer, or Yoruba at home, or French or Fulani with neighbors or at the market. "You are smart," his teacher told him, "to be able to speak so many languages."

Hakeem studied the words. One day he would

go to college in England or the United States. Friends of his parents sent their children to foreign countries to study. They always celebrated with a party. Everyone danced, and Hakeem ate *fufu* from pounded yams and *dodos* from fried bananas until his belly hurt.

Someday his parents would have a party for him. Someday he would leave Lagos.

Someday he would be a famous soccer star like Pelé from Brazil or George Best from England. People all over the world would watch his soccer games on television.

He tried to stop his daydreams and read his lesson. But he did not want books today. He wanted to be outside, running, jumping, kicking the soccer ball as hard as he could, bouncing it off his head and chest.

Like other children in Lagos, Hakeem grew up loving soccer. Soccer is the most popular sport in Nigeria. Toddlers learn to kick; five-year-olds hit balls with their foreheads.

Hakeem, always full of energy, played with his brothers and friends in the sandy field near his home. When he was old enough he joined the school team. He was tall and skinny, but graceful. He ran fast. He kicked the ball, first with the right foot, then with the left foot. He zig-zagged down the field. He bounced it off his head, he dodged back and forth to block shots.

Hakeem was his team's goalie. His job was to keep the other team from scoring. He was good. He was one of the best in the city, then in Nigeria.

The competition inspired him. He learned something that he would repeat over and over during his career in professional sports: work hard, work smart, finish strong.

Eight-year-old Hakeem Olajuwon had tasted winning and he liked it. It was a taste he would never outgrow.

3

Driving Lesson

Hakeem and Akinola knew where their father kept the car keys. They also knew they weren't allowed to take the car. But the brothers wanted to learn to drive.

Hakeem was fifteen. Akinola was fourteen months younger than Hakeem. They were so tall, many people thought they were older. If they could only drive, they could get into parties, and dance and listen to music.

Growing up in Nigeria, the brothers did everything together. They played soccer with the other boys along Bank-olemo, the U-shaped street in front of their house. Lagos was a large city, but everyone knew each other on Bank-olemo.

The Olajuwon brothers and their friends built camps in the forest near their homes. They hunted birds with their slingshots. They had high-jump contests. They were always testing each other. Who was the strongest? Who was the fastest? Who was the best?

Hakeem was the tallest at more than six feet. So he was the leader. The other boys called him a warrior.

They tried to be faster or stronger than he was. But few could beat him. The harder they tried, the more Hakeem worked. He liked the challenge. He liked being best. He liked to win. And he wasn't afraid to work hard to get what he wanted.

On this weekend Hakeem wanted to learn to drive. His parents were visiting with friends, so they didn't notice when Hakeem and Akinola took the car keys.

Quietly the boys crept to the garage. They

pushed the car out without turning it on. No one heard them. When they were a safe distance from home, they jumped in, started the car and drove off.

This first driving lesson did not have a happy ending. Within the next few months, they wrecked two family cars while teaching each other how to drive. The first wreck was that night.

Dad was very angry. "You two are rascals," he said. "Hakeem, you are the oldest. You are responsible for your younger brother. You will pay for the car."

As usual, Mummy protected her boys. She taught them many things. One important lesson was to be independent and to make their own decisions. She did not agree with their decision to borrow the car. But to pay for repairs seemed a harsh punishment. Finally their father agreed.

"She's the best," Akinola said later in their room. Hakeem nodded.

They climbed into their bunkbeds. In loud

whispers they talked about the things brothers talk about everywhere. Music. Girls. Sports. And the next time they could practice driving— after the car was fixed.

An American Dream

The airplane was stuffy and the seat was tiny. Hakeem Olajuwon was seventeen years old. He didn't like sitting still for so long. He didn't have any place to stretch out his long legs or put his size 17 feet.

He tried to be patient. "Patience is a virtue, but it is something you must practice," his parents told him often. But he didn't want to be patient. He wanted to get to America and play basketball.

His older brother Yemi was in school in London. His sister Kudirak attended American University in Cairo. Hakeem was headed to the

United States because an American coach in Africa had seen him play. Christopher Pond's Central African team beat Nigeria in the 1980 All-African Games.

Hakeem was on the team. His high school's basketball coach convinced him to switch from soccer. "You are built for basketball," he said. At sixteen, Hakeem was already six feet nine inches tall.

Pond had seen talent in the young Nigerian. "Go to the United States and play basketball," Pond told Hakeem. He gave Hakeem a list of schools. "You should be able to get a scholarship at one of these."

Now Hakeem was on his way. He beamed with excitement.

No, he didn't know where he would live. No, he didn't know anyone in the big wild nation filled with fast food and big cars, *Star Wars* movies and disco music. And the best basketball players in the world. But the seventeen-year-old knew what he was going to do. He was going to play basketball—get a scholarship so he could go to school free—and get an education. He would study business or law or architecture. Then he would go home to Nigeria and be with his family. He missed them already. His round-trip ticket was good for one year, just in case he changed his mind.

Hakeem's plane landed at John F. Kennedy Airport in New York. St. John's University in Queens, New York, was the first school on his list of schools to visit. But when Hakeem walked off the plane he knew this was not the place for him. October 1980 in New York was freezing cold. No month in Nigeria is freezing cold. Young Hakeem Olajuwon would have none of it. He turned right around, ready for the next school.

The next stop on his ticket was Houston, Texas. An airline attendant got him a seat on the next flight. First the passenger made a telephone call. The phone rang on Guy V. Lewis's desk in the University of Houston's athletic department.

"Hello, Coach. This is Hakeem Olajuwon

calling from New York City. Did anyone tell you about me?''

Lewis knew a tall African kid was on his way to the United States to look over schools. He'd heard the kid was six feet seven inches or so. Young men from far away places were constantly making the rounds to see American basketball coaches. Usually those who claimed to be six feet seven inches were only six feet four inches or shorter. So Coach Lewis did not expect anything special.

But the young Nigerian was a long way from home. He had a plane ticket. ''Come on,'' Lewis told him. ''I'll have somebody meet you at the airport.''

Hakeem climbed aboard another plane and flew west. Coach Lewis got busy and forgot all about the teenager, the plane, and his promise.

A few hours later Lewis's phone rang again. Again it was Hakeem. ''Coach, there is no one here to meet me,'' he said.

''Get a cab and come on in,'' the coach said. When the cab pulled up in front of the athletic department, Lewis looked out to see a giant of a man uncurl himself from the backseat. This man was no six feet four inches. He was almost seven feet tall and weighed 190 pounds. Lewis nearly ran over his two assistants as they rushed outside.

"What a string bean," Lewis thought. "Need to beef him up with some milkshakes and steaks." He reached out to shake hands with the shy, lanky teenager. "Welcome to Houston," he said.

Hakeem looked around him. The weather was warm and humid like the African city he had left only a few hours earlier. He had found his second home.

Learning About
American Basketball

It was a joke. People said Coach Guy V. Lewis recruited new players for the University of Houston basketball team on a bicycle. He didn't. But he could have. All the players were from the Houston area except Lyndon Rose, who was from the Bahamas.

One of Lewis's new recruits in 1981 was Reid Gettys from Memorial High School.

One evening Lewis was at Gettys's house. Gettys had heard about a secret weapon Lewis had up his sleeve. He was curious. "Tell me about the big guy from Africa," he said.

Lewis smiled bigger than the Cheshire cat grinning at Alice in Wonderland. "We think you'll enjoy playing with him. He'll be one of the greatest players you've ever seen," he answered.

Lewis didn't always think that. When he and his Cougars first saw Hakeem walk into the gym, they shook their heads. The seventeen-year-old Hakeem was scared. He was shy. He was overly polite and had a habit of bowing slightly at the end of a conversation. He was a string-bean kid 6,500 miles from home, trying to fit in.

But on the basketball court, he became a different person. There, he was confident. There, he was comfortable. He was the tallest man on the floor. He moved as fast as a rocket. He jumped with the grace of a gazelle.

But he didn't know enough about the American game of basketball. He fouled too much. He didn't know where to stand or where to throw.

Lewis detected some secret ingredient in his lanky new player. What was it? An intense desire to learn? Raw talent? Great instincts? Yes, and more.

Hakeem didn't play with the Cougars his first year in Houston. He got to school after the season started. So instead he watched, listened, and practiced.

Second semester he enrolled in school on a basketball scholarship. During the summer he played every day at Fonde Recreation Center near downtown Houston where college and pro players gather for pickup games.

Clyde Drexler, Michael Young, Larry Micheaux, Lyndon Rose—the UH players were tough competition for the pros in town.

One of the pros was Moses Malone. Moses was the Houston Rockets' center and one of the top players in the NBA.

Day after day Moses whalloped the young Hakeem. Hakeem did not like to lose. So he learned: to block; to position himself for rebounds; to concentrate.

Hakeem started his first season of college basketball on the bench. He didn't like it there. He itched to play, to try the hook shot he learned from Moses, to prove what he could do.

In practice teammates called him Jelly after a player named Joe "Jellybean" Bryant. Hakeem's basketball game wasn't like Bryant's. But Bryant was a clown who could make his teammates laugh. So could Hakeem.

Once, during practice, Gettys took a shot from the top of the key. Hakeem, standing several feet closer to the basket, reached up Supermanlike and snatched the ball in midair. He walked over, handed the ball to Gettys and said, without a smile, "Oh, Reid. Here is your shot."

Gettys didn't know whether to laugh or cry. The block was magic. The blocker was hilarious.

Sometimes people could not tell when Hakeem was being funny. When the team needed an extra push, or hadn't done well in practice, Cougar coaches told players to run laps. Hakeem wanted to shoot baskets, not run laps.

"What, Coach? I do not understand," he said.

Sometimes a coach fell for Hakeem's convenient lapse in understanding the language. But not Lewis, who yelled, "You've been speaking

English as long as I have and you can understand every word I'm saying. Now get out there
and run.''

By the end of the season, Hakeem was starting most games. He played in twenty-nine
games, starting in six.

And he had proved his worth. ''You will start
next year,'' Lewis told his young protégé.

''You're ready to dominate,'' Moses told
him. He laughed to himself. ''Those guys aren't
going to know what hit 'em.''

College Dream

During his years at the University of Houston, Hakeem and the nation changed together.

Computers became common in businesses and homes. *E.T., Raiders of the Lost Ark,* and *Star Trek* were movie hits. *Thriller* by Michael Jackson became the best-selling album of all time. The artificial heart, compact discs, and the world's first reusable space craft, *Columbia,* were invented.

The tall skinny kid from Nigeria became one of the top names in college basketball. He lost some of his accent but none of his charm. He developed a passion for American ice cream.

He practiced every day. He put on muscle, grew another inch. He went from a big bag of potential to a strong self-confident player who would not take bullying—not from Moses Malone—not from anybody.

As a sophomore he played every game. And when he played, fans gasped. They had never seen anything like this. He hooked. He dunked. He played "above the rim." He whirled like the tornado that swept Dorothy and Toto from Kansas to Oz. He swatted opponents' shots right out of the air. He dunked some more.

He blocked more shots than any other college player. He swiped 388 rebounds. He led the University of Houston Cougars to the college basketball championship game three years in a row.

The team was nicknamed "Phi Slama Jama," the world's tallest fraternity. Players included Hakeem, Clyde Drexler, Michael Young, Larry Micheaux, Alvin Franklin, and Reid Gettys. They ruled the Southwest Conference from 1982 to 1984.

And Hakeem was the slammingest, jamming-est of them all. He was 220 pounds of steam-roller. He exploded with energy.

Fans named him The Dream. The nickname stuck. It rhymed. Fans like names that rhyme, like Clyde "The Glide" Drexler and Earl "The Pearl" Monroe.

Fans like symbolism, too. Michael "Air" Jordan hung over the basket and flew across the court. Earvin "Magic" Johnson got his nick-name from a sportswriter who saw a fifteen-year-old score 36 points, get 18 rebounds, and make 16 assists in one game. Karl "The Mail-man" Malone always delivers.

Dream became a symbol for Hakeem. It stood for his journey to Texas and to college super-stardom. It stood for believing in himself.

Professional teams wanted him. Playing pro-fessional ball meant big money. Hakeem de-cided to skip his final year of college play.

He was the No. 1 draft pick, and the Houston Rockets got to choose first. Everybody knew they would pick their hometown college star.

In August 1984 the Rockets signed Hakeem Olajuwon. His six-year contract was worth more than $1 million a year.

Hakeem was excited. The Rockets were excited. Houston was delirious.

Mr. Millionaire Olajuwon bought a white Mercedes-Benz, a big one, with plenty of leg room. He loved his car. It was something he'd dreamed about since he wrecked the family car at age fifteen in Lagos.

He also bought a house with big iron gates with his initials on them and a swimming pool painted like a basketball court. He bought fine clothes, designed his own jewelry. He sent for his younger brothers, who still lived with their parents in Nigeria. Afis was thirteen and Tajudeen fifteen when they moved to Texas. They attended a private high school in Houston; then they went to the University of Texas at San Antonio to play basketball.

The four brothers were finally together. In 1981 Hakeem convinced Akinola, a student at the University of Milan in Italy, to transfer to the University of Houston. "In America you own a car by yourself," Hakeem said.

He and Reid Gettys met one day and decided to shoot baskets. "You ride with me," Hakeem suggested.

Gettys walked out to the parking lot expecting to see the Mercedes. Hakeem pointed to a sleek white Porsche.

"Hey, Jelly. Where's the Benz?" Reid asked.

Hakeem grinned. "My new house has a two-car garage," he said.

Gettys grinned back. Jelly had left the team. Jelly had a million bucks. But Jelly was still Jelly and could make his friends laugh.

7

Dream Shake

The gymnasium is quiet. Two lone men fill the entire court. Their skin sparkles with sweat. Their muscles are strong. They are like tigers stalking dinner, ready to jump and race in a second.

Both are tall and dark. They murmur softly to each other. Hakeem Olajuwon and his youngest brother are practicing basketball in the Second Baptist Church gym. Afis is testing himself against a master. Hakeem is trying out new moves.

He is adding more ingredients to his famous Dream Shake. But this shake has no ice cream.

Sports reporter Michael Murphy of the *Houston Chronicle* described it best: a "mass of twitches, tics, feints, fakes, and drop-steps that lead to so many hook shots, dunks, and fallaway 15-footers."

"It looks a bit like Houdini struggling to get out of a straitjacket," another reporter wrote.

The Dream Shake started out as The Big Step To The Basket.

Guy V. Lewis learned it in the air force. He taught it to the king-sized Cougars at the University of Houston. Elvin Hayes. Ken Spain. Hakeem Olajuwon.

"It's easy to say but so hard to teach," Lewis says. "It starts with a simple thing like catching the ball. You've seen a lot of big guys not pay attention to where the ball is, and when the guards throw it in to them they're not ready for it, and they fumble the ball away. Hakeem very very seldom fumbles the ball away."

Next check the defense. Then step toward the basket.

Lewis added a fourth part. "I always told

them to step to the basket and dunk it," he said. His Cougars were famous dunkers.

Over the years Hakeem added to the Dream Shake recipe. A spoonful of sugar here. A cupful of Tabasco there. A fake here. A fallaway baseline jumpshot there.

Even now, he keeps moving the shake out a few feet. He wants that shooting range. He wants those 3-pointers from 22 feet. Hakeem will never finish the shake. Having the best footwork in the National Basketball Association doesn't mean he can stop working on it.

And who can guard that shot? It's the most effective weapon in basketball today. Coaches try to figure it out. Opponents try to predict when it's coming. Like a blob of mercury, the Dream Shake keeps changing and changing.

Hakeem used one version against David Robinson during the 1994–95 Western Conference Playoffs with the San Antonio Spurs.

It was game two. Moments earlier Robinson had been handed the trophy for the season's Most Valuable Player. But in this game Hakeem was worth more than a pickup truck full of trophies.

He froze Robinson with one Dream Shake, then another, and another. In one, he dribbled, pump-faked left, showed the ball, spun, pumped right, and showed the ball again. Robinson knew a fake was coming. He didn't jump the first time. But he didn't anticipate the second fake and he flew by as Hakeem turned back left and scored two of his 41 points that game.

The Rockets won the game 106 to 96. They won the series.

Afis takes a breather. He learns by watching his brother. He learns how to work hard.

Hakeem has the court by himself. He has no basketball in his hands. Again and again he goes over a move. His face is determined. His feet dance back and forth, left and right, like the magic brooms in Fantasia.

The feet come first, Hakeem says. Without the footwork you can't set up your shot. Your feet take you to the right spot.

''In a soccer game, when you are running to

the ball and somebody's chasing you from behind, you have to misdirect them and control the ball. It is much the same. You want to confuse them," Hakeem tells his brother. His brown eyes fill with fire and humor as he adds, "I just translate it over to basketball. It's nothing much."

Afis can learn footsteps. "But I cannot teach you to be quick and to react," Hakeem says. "You have to develop it to be yours."

The brothers are together again on the court. They spar fiercely. Hakeem slides through the steps he practiced, this time with his brother guarding him.

Step. Step. Turn. Step. Then, in one quick sly whirl, he bobs and shoots from 20 feet. With only a whisper, the ball sinks through the hoop.

Afis makes a face. He likes the Dream Shake more when his brother uses it on Shaquille O'Neal or Patrick Ewing.

Hakeem smiles and slaps his little brother on the shoulder. "It's just a move." He shrugs.

Faith

Abike Olajuwon did not send her son halfway around the world to play basketball. She expected him to get a college education and come home.

But he stayed. He left college early. He became an instant millionaire.

How can a person make that much money playing sports? she wondered.

Hakeem sent videotapes of Rockets games. His mother trembled when he fell or argued with a referee. She smiled when he made a basket and the crowd cheered. His father learned to understand the game. School children all over

Nigeria played basketball because of their son. As parents of Africa's most famous athlete, the Olajuwons are recognized and admired in their country.

The Olajuwons are proud that their son has always been a hero. The Rockets always won.

But that was before NBA games scores were telecast worldwide. Now Hakeem's family knows that the Rockets don't always win. The Olajuwons have retired from their successful cement business. Each year they travel to Houston and stay in a townhouse Hakeem has for them. If they visit during basketball season, they watch Hakeem's games on TV. They don't like the crowds or the noise. They have never seen their superstar son play a game in person.

In Houston they see four of their children. Akinola and Afis are business partners. Tajudeen works with Hakeem's company, Barakaat Holding.

Slowly Abike Olajuwon has become used to her second son's fame and wealth.

Hakeem signed a four-year $25.4 million contract with the Rockets. He gets paid for endorsing products like gym shoes, computers, and tacos. He dines with famous actors and politicians. He talks with David Letterman on late-night television. Letterman called him "the gentle giant."

Abike Olajuwon is most happy that her son is a good Muslim.

At college in America, he embraced American ways. He left some of his Muslim ways at home. But his parents taught him well. In 1991 Hakeem and Akinola traveled to Mecca, the religious center of Islam, in Saudi Arabia. There, twenty-eight-year-old Hakeem rededicated himself to Islam.

Islam is a religion much like Judaism and Christianity. All three believe in one God. Muslims call God *Allah*.

Muslims believe that fourteen centuries ago God gave the prophet Muhammad a message. Muhammad wrote it in the *Quran* or Koran. It guides Muslims on how to act with prayer, money, education, government, everything.

To be a Muslim is to live your whole life by these guidelines. Most important are The Five Pillars of Islam. Following them takes discipline. That's the point.

The first is faith. It means that Muslims should not be tempted to put anything like power or money before God.

The second is prayer or *salat*. Muslims perform prayer five times a day: dawn, noon, midafternoon, sunset, and nightfall. Hakeem often prays before games when the national anthem plays.

The third is called *zakat* or charity.

The fourth is fasting. In a special month in the Islamic calendar called Ramadan, Muslims are not supposed to eat or drink during daylight.

This is very difficult for Hakeem when Ramadan falls during the basketball season, especially during afternoon games when he does not even drink water. One February he lost ten pounds during the fast. During the New York Knicks game in 1995, he became so dehydrated he quit sweating.

"You learn to appreciate the gifts God gives us, even something as simple as a glass of water," he said.

Fasting demonstrates that you are a good Muslim who can discipline himself, and Hakeem is a good Muslim.

The last pillar is called *hajj*. It is a trip or pilgrimage to Mecca. Mecca (or *Makkah* in Arabic) is Muhammad's hometown. In the town, which is surrounded by desert, is the Shrine of Ka'ba. Muslims believe this is the spot where Abraham built the first House of God more than 4,000 years ago. All Muslims face toward Ka'ba when they pray.

Pilgrims traveling to Mecca wear special clothes to remind them that everyone is equal before God.

When Hakeem and Akinola made the *hajj*, they dressed in white sheets of cloth, one around their waists, another around their shoulders. They shaved their heads. Other pilgrims could not tell one was a famous basketball star and one was a successful businessman.

Hakeem Olajuwon talks about his faith, he practices his faith, and he lives his faith. He walks the talk.

He no longer gets kicked out of games for fighting or arguing with officials. ''Powerful is not he who knocks the other down, indeed powerful is he who controls himself in a fit of anger,'' wrote Muhammad.

Hakeem donates time and money to help his community. And he became a U.S. citizen on April 2, 1993.

When he was asked to endorse basketball shoes, Hakeem decided on a company that would make a Hakeem model for about $50. He couldn't understand why basketball players have to be associated with shoes that cost $150. Most kids can't afford that.

Abike Olajuwon may never understand why Americans are so crazy about basketball. Or why her son gets paid so much for playing a game. But she understands his success. After all, he has a strong faith and strong Yoruba ancestors.

Mr. MVP

Nobody is counting. But it looks like every one of the 16,611 seats in The Summit is empty. Every person in The Summit is standing up. Every person in The Summit will have a sore throat tomorrow. They are chanting with all their might: "MVP. MVP. MVP."

The red Rockets and the purple Utah Jazz are ready to start Game 2 of the 1993–94 Western Conference finals in Houston.

But first, NBA commissioner David Stern takes over. He stands midcourt, holding a big bronze trophy.

Hakeem Olajuwon, dressed in the Rockets'

white warmup pants and jacket, walks onto the court to join him.

"MVP. MVP." The chant gets louder.

Stern speaks into the microphone. "I'm here representing millions of basketball fans from around the world. You have had a fantastic NBA career and have led your team to their best season ever. You are a certain Hall of Famer, and you do it with an elegance and grace that is spectacular. Congratulations on being the Most Valuable Player in the NBA."

He presents the trophy to Hakeem. Hakeem nods to his teammates and coaches. They join him on the floor.

The basketball world gasps. Nobody can remember an MVP sharing this spotlight before.

Hakeem hands the trophy to Otis Thorpe. Thorpe hands it back to him. He gives it to Vernon Maxwell. Maxwell places it on the floor in front of the team.

"Thank you and all praises to God," Hakeem says into the microphone to the stunned crowd. "I would like to extend my gratitude to the fans

The University of Houston introduces Hakeem Olajuwon in January 1981.

(Photo by Steve Ueckert/ Houston Chronicle)

University of Houston freshman Hakeem Olajuwon.

(Photo by Steve Ueckert/ Houston Chronicle)

As part of Black History Month Hakeem Olajuwon talked about African heritage with sixty fourth- and fifth-graders from Hartsford Elementary School at the Museum of Fine Arts in Houston. He was honorary chairman of the exhibition called Benin: Royal Art of Africa, February 23, 1994.

(Photo by Steve Ueckert/ Houston Chronicle)

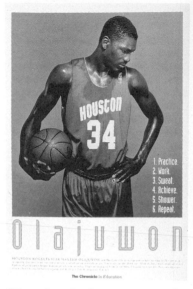

1. Practice.
2. Work.
3. Sweat.
4. Achieve.
5. Shower.
6. Repeat.

Olajuwon

The Chronicle In Education

When the University of Houston photographed its 1984 Phi Slama Jama team, all five players had to jump at one time. They didn't rely on fancy computer work to put the individual photos together. The basket was raised several feet so Hakeem's hand wasn't above the basket. Players are (*from left*): Hakeem Olajuwon, Michael Young, Alvin Franklin, Eric Dickens, and Reid Gattys.

(Photo courtesy of the University of Houston)

Education is important to the Rockets All-Star. He posed for this photograph for the *Houston Chronicle*'s Newspaper in Education program.

(Photo by Arthur Myerson)

Rockets center Hakeem Olajuwon and Utah's Karl Malone prove why professional athletes have to be in good condition as they go after the ball in a 1987 game.

(Photo by Dave Einsel/ Houston Chronicle)

Co-captains Clyde Drexler and Hakeem Olajuwon watched the 1995 National Basketball Association world championship banner unfurl at the Rockets first home game of the 1995–96 season. The trophy sat on a black pedestal in the center court during the flashy ceremony.

(Photo by Smiley N. Pool/ Houston Chronicle)

Hakeem Olajuwon returned to the Summit court for the first time since a January 3 eye injury on March 5, 1991.

(Photo by Kerwin Plevka/ Houston Chronicle)

A little Dream Shake bamboozles the San Antonio Spurs.

(Photo by Paul Howell/ Houston Chronicle)

Hakeem takes a big step to the basket against Shaquille O'Neal. They compete fiercely on the court and are friends off the court.

(Photo by Kerwin Plevka/ Houston Chronicle)

Sometimes Hakeem tops off his Dream Shake with a monster jam like this one against the Spurs in the 1995 conference playoffs.

*(Photo by Paul Howell/*Houston Chronicle*)*

Every year Abike and Salam Olajuwon travel from Nigeria to visit their Houston sons. Gathered at the town house Hakeem keeps for them are (*from left*): Akinola, Abike, Tajudeen, Salam, and Afis; an older brother and sister live in Lagos. This photo was taken in 1994 when the Olajuwons stayed after the NBA Championships to attend Akinola's wedding.

(Photo by David Fahleson/ Houston Chronicle)

Tami Mendiola greets Hakeem Olajuwon with tears when he went to Black Middle School in Houston to talk about the importance of education on February 22, 1995.

(Photo by Ben DeSoto/ Houston Chronicle)

Hakeem Olajuwon, his daughter, Abisola, and his parents, Abike and Salam, celebrated his being named Most Valuable Player in the NBA on June 26, 1994, at a party given by his brother Akinola. More than 300 guests were served caviar and non-alcoholic drinks.

(Photo by Richard Carson/ Houston Chronicle)

At last buddies Hakeem Olajuwon and Clyde Drexler win a championship together. The team helped design the prized rings; each has thirty-three diamonds.

(Photo by Steve Ueckert/ Houston Chronicle)

The second championship trophy was even sweeter than the first. *Two-rrific!* screamed newspaper headlines and television sportscasters. Mario Elie kisses the Larry O'Brian trophy as Clyde and Hakeem enjoy the jubilation.

(Photo by Smiley N. Pool/ Houston Chronicle)

Professional basketball athletes play more than eighty games a season, so they learn to rest their hard-working muscles whenever they can. Hakeem, Clyde Drexler, and Charles Jones relax during practice between games of the 1995 NBA finals.

(Photo by *Howard Castleberry/* Houston Chronicle)

Abby Olajuwon and her superstar dad ride on top of a fire engine as the parade for the champions wound through Houston. Behind Hakeem is "Granny" Wert.

Houston Rockets center Hakeem Olajuwon smiles while sporting the red, white, and blue U.S. Olympic jersey for the first time in Secaucus, New Jersey, August 1995. For Olajuwon being one of the first ten players selected for the twelve-man 1996 Olympic team marked the end of one mission and the start of another—winning a gold medal.

(AP photo/Joe Tabacca)

of Houston. And as you know, this is a team sport, so I also would like to extend my gratitude to my teammates. And also my coaches. Thank you very much.''

Fans stomp and scream. They cry and cheer. They make more noise than a rocketship lifting off at Cape Canaveral. They love this tall humble man. They love his style. They love his determination and his dignity. They love him because he is a great player. But most of all they love him because he is theirs.

''It felt wonderful. It felt so warm. It felt like an embrace,'' Hakeem said.

And the fellas in the purple uniforms? They stand politely at their end of the court. It does not look like a good night for the Utah Jazz. It isn't. They had already lost Game 1.

Tonight the Jazz cannot stop Mr. MVP. They put two men on his every move. He still shoots and hits. They put three men on him. Shoot. Hit.

Dream gives fans a dream night. He wraps Game 2 in a pretty package with 41 points, 13 rebounds, and 6 assists inside. Victory: 104 to 99.

"If they didn't have Superman, we'd have won that game," Jazz guard Jeff Hornacek says after the game. "We had guys in his way and he throws up shots that are unreal."

After the game Hakeem is ready to get home. He likes the roar of crowds. He thrives on the feel of the varnished floor under his feet and the ball in his hands. He loves competing and winning and knowing he and his teammates can operate with the precision and smoothness of his big car. But he cherishes his home. It is, he likes to say, a Muslim home. There is no noise. There are no flashy spotlights, glaring red and yellow colors. It is white, calm, and elegant. Inside it is peaceful, like the owner himself.

Hakeem helped design this house. Tall ceilings give him space. Big windows make the big rooms bright and airy. He doesn't feel boxed in here.

A shiny black baby grand piano sits in one airy room. Hakeem's art collection hangs on the walls. His closets are full of beautiful fabrics and rich elegant colors. One of his unofficial titles is "best dressed" man in the NBA.

Alongside elegant suits hang traditional Nigerian matching pants and caftans. Because he is so tall, many of his clothes are made specially for him. Hakeem has had a passion for beautiful clothes since he was a child. His mother rewarded her children by buying them clothes and shoes.

There are few clues that this home belongs to a world-famous basketball player.

But a new clue has just arrived. "Where," Hakeem thinks as he wanders from room to room, "shall I put my new trophy?"

Dreams of Championships

The sun has not announced morning when Hakeem's eyes snap open. His house is quiet, still. He likes it that way.

His life is often filled with roars and silences. He cannot imagine his life without the crowds. Nor can he imagine his life without the precious quiet time when he can think, read, and pray.

This morning he feels extra pressure. Today he and the Rockets face one of their toughest tests.

He knows Coach Rudy Tomjanovich's prime directive: the open man gets the ball. He closes his eyes and reruns plays in his mind. Yes, Hakeem whispers into the dark. His muscles ache for action. He feels the ball in his hands, feels it leave his fingers and fly like a falcon.

Yes, he whispers again.

It is 5:30 and time for morning prayer.

When he's traveling, he uses a compass to point east to Mecca. But at home he knows which direction to face. He kneels on his prayer rug and begins. It takes about five minutes. But even those five minutes calm him. "Focus," he tells himself. "Concentrate. For today I must be strong."

Tonight the Rockets play for the NBA championship. They face the New York Knicks. The Rockets have won three games in the best-of-seven finals. The Knicks have won three games. Except in Houston, most people think the Knicks will win Game 7 and the championship trophy.

For the seventh time in less than two weeks he will square off against Knicks's center Patrick Ewing. Hakeem and Patrick are old rivals. In 1984 they played for the NCAA championship. Then it was the University of Houston vs. Georgetown University. Ewing's team won.

"We both play to win, but he won't win tonight," Hakeem said to himself. He flicked on the VCR and again studied the tape of Ewing in action.

Dikemba Mutombo of the Denver Nuggets knows both men. He went to Georgetown University like Ewing. He is from Africa like Olajuwon. "They both deserve it so much. They have both waited so long," he said before the championship game. "It is as if two men have been in the desert and they come upon one glass of water. There is only enough for one of them to drink. When you watch them, do you not wish there could be two glasses of water?"

Like other team members, Hakeem takes an afternoon nap. His mind and muscles must be alert. He must rest.

That night millions of people in seventeen countries tune their television sets to the game. They watch Hakeem. They watch Ewing.

The team which makes the fewest mistakes wins, assistant coach Carroll Dawson says. Hakeem is determined to make no mistakes.

Hakeem and the Rockets play their best. Positive. Confident. Tough as kryptonite.

Three times in the final minutes of Game 7, the Knicks surrounded Hakeem. He cannot move. But each time he finds an open man. He throws the ball, his teammate shoots. Two points.

The final score: 90 to 84.

The Summit shook with hollering. Hakeem Olajuwon and the Houston Rockets have won their first NBA championship.

At one end of the court, Hakeem clutched the ball to his chest and stood quietly. So this is how it felt. So this was his destiny.

Hakeem the Dream made history. He was the first player to win the championship and to be named regular season Most Valuable Player, Defensive Player of the Year, and MVP of the finals. ''If you write a book, you can't write it any better,'' he said.

He had never seen such celebration. Sam Cassell's grin looked bigger than his face. Kenny Smith cut down the net and hung it around his neck. Robert Horry and Mario Elie gave every-one in sight sweaty hugs.

Hakeem spotted his daughter Abby and swooped her up. He gave her a championship hug. She gave him one back. They wore matching grins.

Owner Leslie Alexander accepted the 1994 championship trophy from basketball commissioner David Stern.

For an instant Hakeem thought of his childhood in Nigeria. He was a warrior. Each day brought somebody who was younger, faster, stronger, to challenge him. Now he and the Rockets are champions. But next year teams will try harder to be younger, faster, stronger, to challenge the champions.

And the Dream will be ready for them.

Dream Off the Court

Tears the size of gumdrops rolled down Tami Mendiola's cheeks. She held her breath. She bit her bottom lip. She thought about her science test. But she couldn't stop them.

The tears embarrassed Tami. They baffled Hakeem Olajuwon.

He was visiting a circle of students at Black Middle School in Houston. He was there to announce his Dream Foundation scholarship program.

Teachers had selected Tami and thirty-nine other students to meet with the NBA All-Star. Tami sat on the front row, right in front of Hakeem.

"My parents always taught me that the key to success was an education. It takes a lot of discipline," the master of discipline told Tami and her classmates.

But Tami kept crying.

The foundation was Hakeem's dream. His faith taught him devotion and charity. If you do something good, something good will return to you. It works like a circle. He had wealth, power, happiness. He needed to give some back. Five Houston high school seniors each year would receive up to $4,000 for college. But they have to earn good grades.

"Do you have a dream?" he asked the students. They nodded.

"Not all of us can be NBA basketball players. But all of us can strive for a better education," he told them. They nodded.

"You can accomplish goals through discipline and study," he said quietly. "If you seek knowledge, your dreams will come true."

They nodded. Tami kept crying.

Hakeem looked at the eighth-grader. He

leaned toward her. "Why are you crying?" he asked. "Don't be nervous."

Then he realized what was wrong. Tami wasn't nervous. She was overwhelmed. Here she was, in the same room with the basketball player she and millions of other people worshipped. He was only inches away from her.

Hakeem always tried to make people feel at ease around him. He shook hands, signed basketballs, listened to fans.

But he wasn't used to tears.

"You have to look at everyone as just a human being," he said softly to Tami. "Don't let what you see on TV make you think someone is special or above you. I'm a regular person just like you. I went to the White House last week to meet President Clinton. And I was honored to be there. But I am just as honored to be here with you."

Tami looked up at his face. She saw that he meant what he said. She wouldn't let him down. She would study and ask questions. She would learn and teach others what she learned. She would set goals and work hard. She would do the best she could.

She gave Hakeem a fragile smile. "And I will do something else," she said to herself. "I will tell everyone I met Hakeem Olajuwon." But she wouldn't tell anyone about the tears.

And no matter what he said, she would never believe one thing he said. He is not a regular person.

Dream Daughter

Alon Riskat Abisola Ajoke Olajuwon doesn't look like her father. She is two feet shorter, wiggly, and seven years old. But she has his calm gentle eyes and his quick smile.

Many people call her Abby. Her famous dad calls her ''sweet little one'' or Abisola, which means ''born in wealth'' in Arabic. He also calls her wonderful and beautiful. ''She is what life is all about,'' he says.

At the age when her father was learning English and field hockey in Nigeria, Abisola practices the piano and learns about computers. She plays with Barbie dolls, reads poems and scary stories, works on the school newspaper, and watches Nickelodeon on TV.

She also plays basketball—and well.

Abisola has two rooms. One is in California where she lives with her mother Lita Spencer Richardson, her stepfather Leonard, and Lita's grandmother, Baby Ruth Wert. Everyone calls her Granny. Granny was named after the candy bar.

The California room is pink and full. Abisola's desk is stacked with books and art supplies and a basketball card collection. She knows most of the guys on the cards.

Abby named her fighting blue fish Shaq-foo. Shaquille O'Neal is her pal. He autographed his size 22 shoe and gave it to her. She took it to school one day. Shaq is her second favorite basketball player.

The room is a shrine to her superstar dad. Pictures of Hakeem are everywhere. A No. 34 red and yellow Rockets uniform hangs on her wall in an eight-foot tall frame, a surprise present from Daddy.

Her other room is in Houston, where she was born on July 6, 1988. This room has a big bed and a television set. And lots of books. Hakeem likes to buy books for his child. He liked a book on travelers and explorers so much he bought one for each of her rooms.

Abby also has a red-and-white prayer rug with a compass on it. She faces Mecca and prays. She studies Arabic and the Koran.

Having two rooms is fun most of the time. So is having a superstar for a dad.

Hakeem teaches his daughter soccer. She teaches him to jump on the trampoline.

Abby spends half her time with him, sometimes in Houston, sometimes traveling. Granny always goes with Abby. Granny has lived with Abby for as long as Abby can remember. Lita jokes that she and Hakeem share custody of Abby and of Granny.

Lita is determined that her tall talkative daughter will have a regular childhood. But that's tough to accomplish.

In California she gets to stay up late, even on

a school night, and watch Rockets basketball on television.

Schoolmates and teachers ask about The Dream. But mostly people ask, "Why are you so tall?" Abby politely answers, "Because my Daddy is tall."

In Houston she has a tutor, a piano teacher, and an Arabic teacher.

She was at The Summit cheering when the Rockets won the championship.

She rode in the Rockets' victory parade through downtown Houston. She sat on top of a big red fire truck with the Rockets and Mayor Bob Lanier and his wife, Elyse.

She remembered to bring her purple camera, a birthday present from her mother. She took pictures of the people who were taking pictures of her.

From the snug safe perch on her father's lap, she saw children wearing red and yellow "34" jerseys that hung past their knees. She saw women with Rockets T-shirts pulled over their dresses. Some men wore red and yellow ties.

They shouted and waved and threw little pieces of colored paper all over the streets. It got in her hair and on her lavender dress. She loved the excitement.

I'm glad I don't have to clean this up, she thought.

Half a million people lined the streets and hung out of buildings.

Abby felt proud that her dad could make people so happy. She used to worry about him. "But he doesn't have a job," she told her mother. "He doesn't get dressed up in the morning and leave for the office. All he does is play basketball every day."

"For some people, a very few people, playing basketball is a job," her mother explained.

Abisola thinks about growing up. Maybe she will be a lawyer like her mother. Or maybe she will play basketball like her father. Or collect art or have a fashion business like him. Or maybe she will be a firefighter so she can ride big red trucks all the time.

Whatever she decides to be, Abisola knows

she will be surrounded by love. She knows that she can make dreams come true. For inside her beats the heart of her father, a heart that is strong and gentle, the heart of a champion.

Recurring Dream

Hakeem walks onto the court. On the shiny floor he sees a basketball. It does not belong there, still, resting. It belongs in his hands, bouncing, sailing.

He leans to pick it up. Like a paperclip to a magnet, the ball jumps into his hands. Joy jumps in Hakeem's eyes.

Suddenly his 255-pound body becomes a butterfly fresh from its cocoon. His seven foot frame becomes an eagle, soaring, majestic, strong. He is electricity, a bouncy puppy, a comet.

He dribbles. He shoots. He rebounds. He cannot be still.

That has not changed since his lone journey to the United States in 1980.

But other things have. He no longer scuffles on the court and off. He has learned to control his temper. The team is no longer called Team Hakeem or Hakeem and the Olajuwonettes. He understands teamwork. He has learned about pain.

A terrible face injury during the third quarter of a Chicago Bulls game in 1991 sent him crashing to the floor nearly unconscious. A swinging elbow caught Hakeem just below the right eye, smashing the bone. He was carried out on a stretcher. Eleven days later he had surgery to repair the damage. He missed twenty-five games. There had been other injuries. There will be more. It is the life of a basketball player.

He has wealth. He has fame. Both can cause trouble. Hakeem knows that. He does not get wrapped up in things like becoming a celebrity or making money.

He has peace within his soul.

''If I never play another basketball game, I would be forever grateful for the success I've had in this game," he says. "People have to look at things for what they have, not what they haven't been given. I am thankful for what I've been given in life. The championship is icing on the cake. I've still had the cake no matter what."

Hakeem has one championship. It happened because of the team's chemistry, hard work, hunger for success. It happened because Coach Rudy Tomjanovich is a chemist, a leader. It happened because of the secret ingredient that Coach Lewis sensed fourteen years ago in the young Hakeem Olajuwon.

Rudy T. has his own name for the secret: heart. "That makes him want to be the best and to do whatever it takes to win. But it's so much more special. He's a great person. He really cares about his fellow man."

And he has his friend Drex.

They are practicing at The Summit. Hakeem tosses the ball to Clyde Drexler. Both men giggle like third-graders. They are happy to be playing together again.

Since the Rockets traded for Clyde midseason, the longtime friends have worked magic. They play like teammates are supposed to play, encouraging each other, understanding each other, moving like two wheels on a bicycle. Each important. Each necessary. Moving together yet individually.

"Clyde is a leader. He is very astute," Hakeem said.

"We are the consummate buddies because we know what each other is going to do. It's so instinctive," Clyde said.

They have fun playing basketball. That is another of Hakeem's secrets. "You play because you enjoy playing. You play for fun," he says.

Hakeem's cake is an elegant one. And the icing—that championship—tasted awfully good.

Now Dream wants more.

Pass the icing. With two spoons, please.

Dream Two-rrific

The Rockets did the impossible: They had only the sixth best record in the Western Conference of the NBA in the 1994–95 season. They lost 35 games and won 47. Yet they did it again in the playoffs. First, they beat Utah. Then they beat the San Antonio Spurs. For the second year in a row they headed for the championship series. There they faced Shaquille O'Neal, Penny Hardaway, and their Orlando Magic teammates.

The Magic was young and fierce. But this Rockets team was special. They had an unshakable belief in each other. The tougher the battle, the harder they fought.

- **Game 1**: Hakeem tipped in a Drexler miss with 0.3 seconds left in overtime. Houston, 120. Orlando, 118.

- **Game 2**: Shaq's 33 points wasn't enough to save his team from Hakeem's 34 points, Sam Cassell's 31 points, and Clyde Drexler's 23 points. Houston, 117. Orlando, 106.

- **Game 3**: Robert Horry's 3-pointer with 14.1 seconds left gave Houston a 3-point lead at The Summit. Houston, 106. Orlando, 103.

Now it was game four. Even seven feet two inch, 305-pound, twenty-three-year-old O'Neal couldn't shake the Rockets. They had been here before. They knew how winning felt. They hungered to repeat.

And they never doubted. Millions watching on television and fans packed into The Summit didn't doubt either.

In the final seconds, Hakeem, on a pass from his college buddy Drex, hit a three-pointer.

Bzzzzz. The horn sounded. The score flashed. Houston Rockets, 113. Orlando Magic, 101. Hakeem scored 35 points.

It was a sweep. The Rockets won all four games of the NBA finals. Only four other teams ever won back-to-back championships. But nobody had ever done it coming off such a disappointing season.

"How sweet it is," the announcer screamed. "How sweet it is."

The crowd hooted like a jungle full of howler monkeys. Red and yellow confetti fell like rain after a hurricane. Fireworks boomed from the rafters like a Fourth of July celebration.

Hakeem sat down and put his face in a towel. He sat perfectly still. It had been a long season. One with more ups and downs than a roller coaster. But now it was time to celebrate. "Thank you," he whispered.

Teammates and coaches slapped Hakeem's back. He and Clyde Drexler hugged like long lost brothers. Finally. Finally, they won together, a dozen years after they lost that college championship game in the last instant.

The first big win brought such joy. But the second was even sweeter. Hakeem could share it with Clyde. Dream and the Glide—together as champions.

Rings

Suddenly the lights in The Summit go out. It is November. It is the Rockets' first game of the 1995–96 season against the Golden State Warriors.

Tonight is no ordinary game night. The team has new colors and new uniforms. Blue replaces yellow with a bit of Rockets red. The court has a new floor painted with the new logo: a fiery rocketship blasting off.

But tonight is more special than that. Tonight Hakeem, his teammates, and the fans will relive that night on June 14, 1995. Tonight the Rockets get their rings. Two NBA championships.

Two championship rings. Two final MVP awards for Hakeem.

He is headed to the 1996 Summer Olympics in Atlanta to be on Dream Team III. Will an Olympic gold medal be added to his growing trophy collection?

Music, a laser show, and twirling spotlights fill the dark arena. One by one, each Rocket walks to the center of the court to get his ring.

Tim Breaux. Charles Jones. Pete Chilcutt. Chucky Brown. Sam Cassell. Kenny Smith. Mario Elie. Robert Horry. Clyde Drexler. Each shakes hands with Rudy T.

Then the announcer takes a deep breath. His voice echoes through the building: "The most popular basketball player on the planet . . . Hakeem Oooo-lajuwon."

Film clips of Hakeem's 1994–95 season flash on the big screens near The Summit ceiling.

A laser show beams "Olajuwon" on the new blue and red floor. Pow. Pow. Fireworks sprinkle stardust in the Summit sky.

Spotlights swirl around his head, one aimed

at him and the little wooden box holding his ring.

It is platinum, not gold like the other rings. Because of his Islamic beliefs, Hakeem does not wear gold jewelry. Rockets management ordered another precious metal for their superstar center.

The ring weighs the same as thirty-one pennies. Carved on top are the two championship trophies set in nine diamonds. Each diamond represents a game the Rockets won on the road during the playoffs. They won nine games in a row. On one side is "Olajuwon," a heart with the Rockets logo in it, then his number, "34."

Hakeem smiles. Fans clap and roar. The Summit is noisier than the inside of a volcano.

Standing in the middle of the celebration, the big man from Nigeria thinks of his friend Clyde and feels a little happier.

He thinks of his daughter and smiles a little bigger.

He thinks of his faith and feels a little stronger.

He thinks of his teammates and holds his head a little higher.

At that moment the man with the big hands holds a whole nation.

At that moment the man with the large feet has traveled far.

The Dream Man is living his dream.

The Dream Man makes dreams come true.

IF YOU DARE TO BE SCARED...
READ SPINETINGLERS!
by M.T. COFFIN

(#1) THE SUBSTITUTE CREATURE
77829-7/$3.50 US/$4.50 Can

(#2) BILLY BAKER'S DOG WON'T STAY BURIED
77742-8/$3.50 US/$4.50 Can

(#3) MY TEACHER'S A BUG
77785-1/$3.50 US/$4.50 Can

(#4) WHERE HAVE ALL THE PARENTS GONE?
78117-4/$3.50 US/$4.50 Can

(#5) CHECK IT OUT—AND DIE!
78116-6/$3.50 US/$4.50 Can

(#6) SIMON SAYS, "CROAK!"
78232-4/$3.50 US/$4.50 Can

(#7) SNOW DAY
78157-3/$3.50 US/$4.50 Can

(#8) DON'T GO TO THE PRINCIPAL'S OFFICE
78313-4/$3.50 US/$4.99 Can

(#9) STEP ON A CRACK
78432-7/$3.50 US/$4.99 Can